D0811544

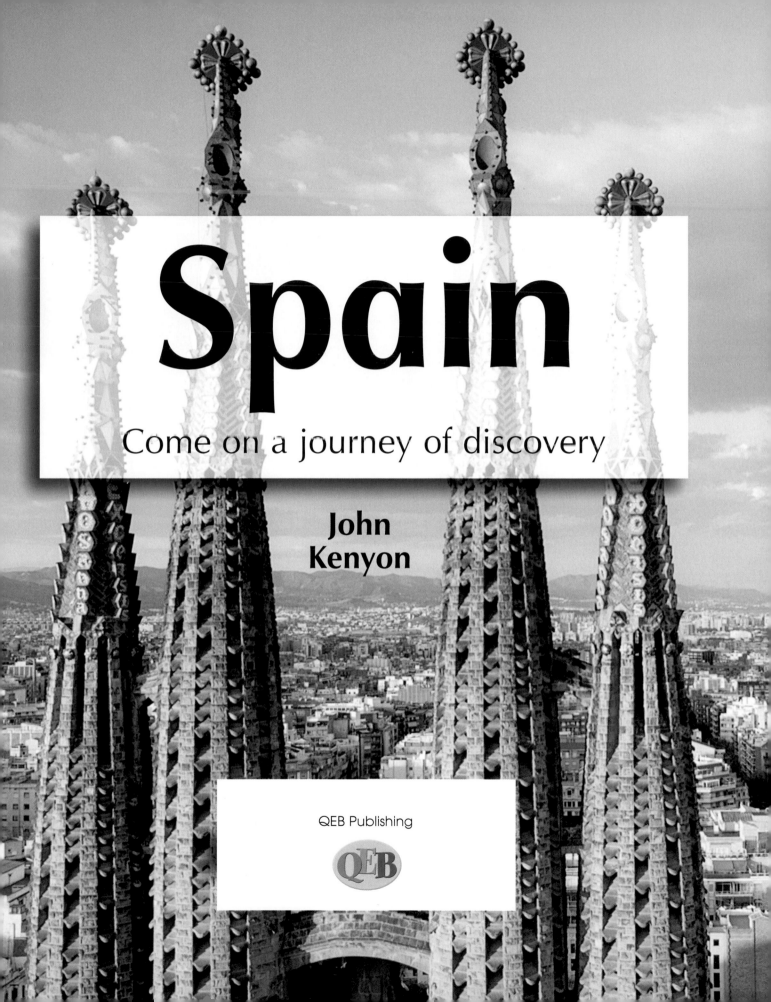

Spain

Come on a journey of discovery

John
Kenyon

QEB Publishing

QEB

Copyright © QEB Publishing, Inc. 2004

Published in the United States by
QEB Publishing
23062 La Cadena Drive
Laguna Hills
Irvine
CA 92653

All rights reserved. No part of this publication may be reproduced, stored in a retrieval system, or transmitted in any form or by any means, electronic, mechanical, photocopying, recording, or otherwise, without the prior permission of the publisher, nor be otherwise circulated in any form of binding or cover other than that in which it is published and without a similar condition being imposed on the subsequent purchaser.

Library of Congress Control Number: 2004101783

ISBN 1-59566-061-5

Written by John Kenyon
Designed by Starry Dog Books Ltd
Editor Christine Harvey
Map by PCGraphics (UK) Ltd

Creative Director Louise Morley
Editorial Manager Jean Coppendale

Picture credits

Key: t = top, b = bottom, m = middle, c = center,
l = left, r = right

Corbis Krist J. Black 12tr,/ Francesc Muntada 14–15,/ Jose Luis Palaez 15br,/ Attal Serge 18bl,/ Gunter Marx 19br,/ Reuters 20–21,/ Paul Almasy 21 br,/ 26–27 Yann Arthus-Bertrand,/ O. Alamany and E. Vicens 26bl, 27tr;
Spanish Tourist Board 3t,/ J. J. Pascual Lobo 3m;
Getty Pete Adams 1,/ Robert Frerck 6m,/ James Strachan 8–9,/ Ian Shaw 9br,/ Doug Armand 13tr,/ Gerard Loucel 22–23,/ Frank Herholdt 24br,/ Rudolf Pigneter 24–25;
Art Directors and TRIP M. Feeney 7m,/ H. Rogers 8bl, 16–17, 22t,/ T. Bognar 10–11,/ B. Turner 10–11c, 19t,/ J. Dallet 12–13, 23tr,/ D. Houghton 17tl,/ Viesti Collection 17tr.

Printed and bound in China

Words in **bold** can be found in the Glossary on page 28.

Contents

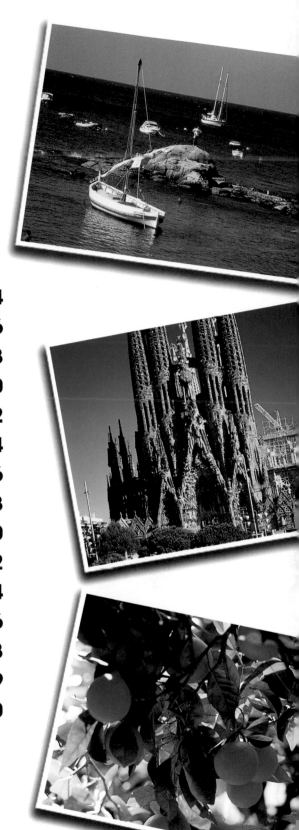

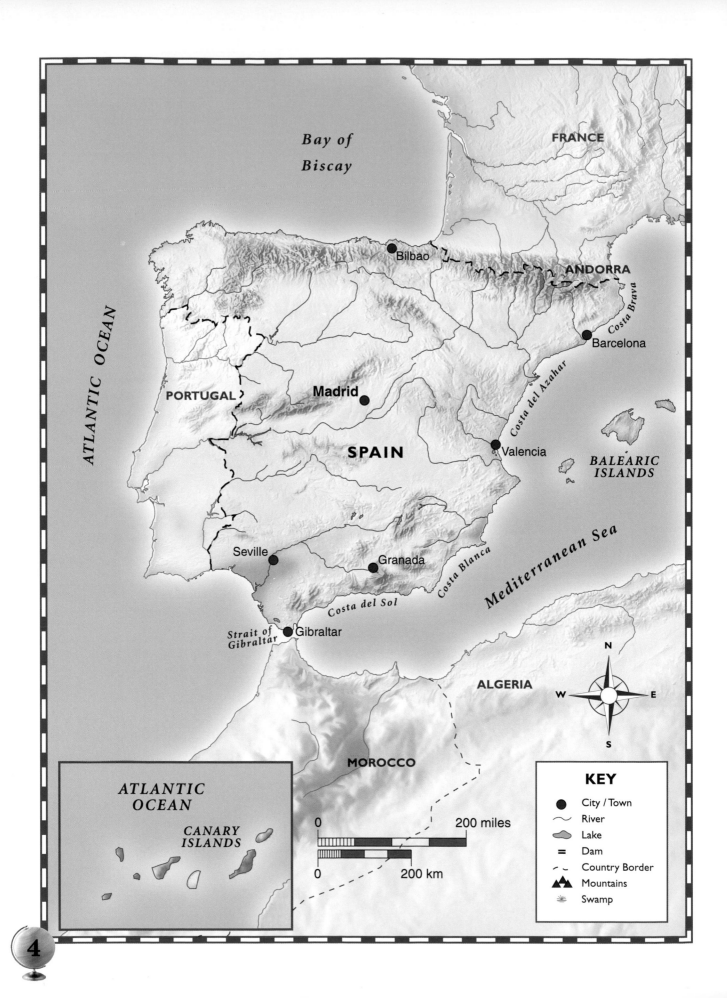

Bay of Biscay

FRANCE

ATLANTIC OCEAN

Bilbao

ANDORRA

Costa Brava

Barcelona

PORTUGAL

Madrid

Costa del Azahar

SPAIN

Valencia

BALEARIC ISLANDS

Seville

Granada

Costa Blanca

Mediterranean Sea

Costa del Sol

Strait of Gibraltar

Gibraltar

ALGERIA

N
W   E
S

MOROCCO

ATLANTIC OCEAN

CANARY ISLANDS

0   200 miles

0   200 km

KEY

● City / Town

～ River

🗾 Lake

= Dam

- - - Country Border

▲▲ Mountains

🌿 Swamp

4

Where in the world is Spain?

Spain is part of the **continent** of Europe. It sits on a large **peninsula** called the Iberian Peninsula. Three countries share borders with Spain. To the north is France, to the northeast is Andorra, and to the west is Portugal.

More than 40 million people live in Spain, and it has the fifth largest population of all the countries in Europe. Spain is about twice as big as the state of Oregon.

Most people who live in Spain speak Spanish. The language was brought to Latin America several hundred years ago by explorers from Spain.

▼ Spain and its place in the world.

Spain

▲ Spain's national flag

Did you know?

Name Spain
Location Southwestern Europe
Neighboring countries France, Portugal and Andorra
Neighboring oceans and seas Mediterranean Sea, Atlantic Ocean, Bay of Biscay
Length of coastline 3,084 miles
Capital Madrid
Area 194,855 square miles
Population 40,217,413
Average life expectancy Male and female: 79 years
Religion 94 percent of the population is Catholic
Languages Castilian Spanish is the official language
Climate Central Spain: hot summers and cold winters; northern coastal areas: mild climate; eastern and southern areas: warm, wet winters and hot, dry summers
Highest mountain range Sierra Nevada
Major rivers Tagus (length: 625 miles), Ebro (length: 565 miles), Duero (length: 556 miles), Guadiana (length: 483 miles), Guadalquivir (length: 408 miles)
Currency Euros (previously pesetas)

What is Spain like?

▼ Old-fashioned windmills are still used to make flour in the Meseta, the central plateau of Spain.

Spain's regions
The **mainland** of Spain is divided into 17 different regions. Each region has its own capital city and its own culture and traditions.

The north
The northeastern part of Spain has a range of mountains called the Pyrenees. They stretch for 280 miles. This mountain range marks the border between Spain and France.

The west
The northern and western **coasts** of Spain face the Atlantic Ocean. This coast has rocky **inlets** called rias.

The Meseta and central Spain

The largest area of Spain is on a high **plateau** called the *Meseta* which spreads for hundreds of miles from the center of Spain. It covers about 40 percent of Spain's land area. The capital city, Madrid, is located right in the middle of the country.

Eastern and southern Spain

Spain has more than 2,000 beaches. Most of them are located in the eastern and southern parts of Spain along the coast of the Mediterranean Sea. Millions of people come to these areas from other European countries to enjoy vacations on the warm, sunny beaches. Barcelona, Spain's second-largest city, is located on the east coast.

▲ In summer, vacationers from other European countries head for Spain's Mediterranean coast to enjoy the warm weather and beaches.

Climate

Spain has a larger land area than most European countries, and if you travel through Spain, you will notice that the weather in different parts of the country varies quite a lot.

Francesca lives in Madrid. Her American pen pal asked her to describe what the weather is like there.

Central Spain

The central plateau of Spain is hot in the summer and cold in the winter. There is only a small amount of rainfall during the year.

Madrid can reach temperatures as high as 103°F in the summer and as low as 5°F in the winter.

The Mediterranean coastline

The east and southeast of Spain lie along the Mediterranean Sea. These areas have hot summers and warm winters. The southern inland region of Andalusia is the hottest and driest part of Europe.

In the summertime, Madrid is really hot, especially at noon. School has a two-hour break in the afternoon and I go home for lunch. After lunch, I usually keep cool by staying home until it is time to go back to school. Sometimes, if it is not too hot, I go out and play with my friends.

In the winter, it gets cold and I have to wear a warm coat when I'm walking to school or if I go out to visit a friend. And the church is so cold on Sunday mornings!

AVERAGE TEMPERATURES ACROSS SPAIN (°F)

	Jan	Feb	March	April	May	June	July	Aug	Sept	Oct	Nov	Dec
Bilbao (northern)	54	55	59	61	66	72	77	77	75	68	61	55
Seville (southern)	52	54	57	61	66	73	81	81	77	66	59	52
Madrid (central)	41	47	48	52	59	68	75	75	68	57	48	43

▲ The cities mentioned on this chart are on the map on page 4.

▼ Temperatures in Madrid, the Spanish capital city, vary a lot between summer and winter. Summers are very hot and winters can be freezing at night.

Carlos lives in the eastern part of Spain, in a city called Benidorm which is popular with tourists. He is writing to his American pen pal about the weather.

Benidorm is warm all year round. It can get hot in the summer. In the winter, it is cooler and this is when most of the rain falls. I prefer the fall when there are fewer tourists and the beaches are not as crowded. Then I can play on the beach with my friends.

Scott Collins
111 Main Street
Somertown, MD 21401
U.S.A.

9

Mountains and rivers

Mountains in the north and south

Some parts of Spain are mountainous. The highest mountain ranges are found in the north and south of the country. The Pyrenees lie in the north.

The mountains in the south are called the Sierra Nevada. They are near the resort towns along the Mediterranean Sea coast. Both ranges have mountains that reach over 11,400 feet above sea level.

Central Spain's mountains

The *Meseta*, Spain's central **plateau**, is surrounded by mountain ranges. Even though it can be very hot in the lower-lying plains of the Meseta, some of the higher mountain peaks have snow on them all year. There are ski resorts in the Guadarrama mountains northwest of Madrid.

▼ Skiing is a popular sport in the Pyrenees mountain range.

Spain's main rivers

There are five main rivers in Spain. Their **sources** are all in the mountain ranges in the Meseta. Four of the rivers flow westward into the Atlantic Ocean. One of these, the Tagus, is the longest river in Spain. The fifth river, the Ebro, flows eastward into the Mediterranean Sea.

The Guadalquivir River

It gets so hot in the Meseta that all the rivers can run dry in places. The most important river is the Guadalquivir, because it is used for river transportation and to irrigate farmland. The river flows through Seville, which is Spain's only port that is on a river, rather than the coast.

◄ Seville is located on the Guadalquivir river.

Did you know?

The highest mountain in mainland Spain is Mulhacen (11,432 feet) in the Sierra Novadas.

The Canary Islands, off the northwest coast of Africa, are also part of spain.

The highest mountain in Spain is Pico de Teide, on the island of Tenerife in the Canary Islands. It is 12,200 feet high.

▼ This map shows Spain's mountain ranges and major rivers.

Getting around Spain

Traveling by air

Air travel is the fastest-growing form of transportation in Spain. The country's increased popularity among tourists has encouraged cheap flights into and out of Spanish airports. There are airports near all the major cities in Spain.

Traveling by road

As Spain developed into an **industrialized** nation, a modern road system became necessary. Trucks and cars needed to be able to travel quickly between cities and towns. There is a system of modern highways called *carretreras* and a network of expressways known as *autopistas*. If you travel through Spain by car, you have to pay a **toll** to use the expressways.

Traffic pollution

The increased traffic in towns and cities has caused air pollution from vehicles. Cities like Barcelona and Madrid have tried to reduce this problem by improving public transportation, such as bus and train services. Many towns also have streetcars, or trams, that go along the main streets.

▲ Some workers in Madrid use the subway system to get to work, instead of driving.

Traveling by train

Spain has one of the most technologically advanced railroad networks in Europe, called the AVE. It uses high-speed tilting trains that can travel up to 200 miles per hour. The high-speed train line connects Seville in southern Spain with Madrid, and it takes less than three hours to travel between these cities. The same trip would take over six hours by car.

▲ Traffic jams in cities can lead to air pollution from vehicles.

Amazing, but true!

The Romans built the first road system in Spain when they ruled there from 200 BC.

Spain has the highest road in Europe. It is in the Sierra Nevada mountains in Andalusia and is 11,470 feet above sea level.

The major highways all start from Madrid in the center of Spain.

◄ The AVE is one of the fastest trains in the world.

Traveling around the regions of Spain

The history of the regions

Spain is made up of 17 regions. Originally, these were all small countries that were united in the 15th century under King John II and King Ferdinand of Aragon. Many Spanish people like to identify themselves as citizens of a particular region, rather than of Spain.

Popular tourist regions

The regions of Catalonia, Valencia, Murcia and Andalusia are the areas that many tourists visit to enjoy the hot weather and beaches in the summer. Barcelona, the second-largest city in Spain, is in Catalonia. Many of the old castles in Catalonia have been preserved and are popular tourist attractions.

▶ Spain is rich in history and there are many well-preserved castles to visit.

Madrid is in Castile Leon, which means "land of the castle." To the northeast, the regions of Navarre and Aragon border France.

In the north-central part of Spain, many of the people are fiercely independent and do not want to be part of Spain. This area is known as the Basque country.

Languages

The official version of Spanish that is spoken in Spain is called Castilian. People in Spain use some different words and have a different accent than Spanish-speaking people from Latin America.

The regions also keep their own traditional languages alive. The other main languages spoken are Catalan in Catalonia; Galician, which is spoken in Galicia in northwest Spain; and Euskera (the Basque language) in the Basque country.

Anna lives in Valencia. She wrote in her diary about an annual festival in the region.

Today was the tomato-throwing festival to celebrate the harvesting of tomatoes in the region. We all had a lot of fun running around the streets throwing tomatoes at each other! I got hit so many times that I was covered in tomato juice. It was even in my shoes and socks!

Traveling through agricultural Spain

Farming
If you travel through some Spanish villages, you might still see farmers using old-fashioned, small-scale methods of farming. During the past thirty years, a lot of small village farmers have been replaced by businesses that use modern farming machinery.

The climate
The choice of crops that can be grown in Spain depends on the climate. Traveling around the regions, you will see different crops growing, depending on the weather and rainfall.

The north
The wet areas in northern Spain are good for growing fruit, such as apples, pears, plums, melons, and peaches. There are also large areas of **grazing land** for cattle, to provide meat and milk.

◄ Spain produces a large quantity of onions, which it exports around the world.

▼ Spain is one of the world's largest producers of wine.

Central Spain
Irrigation makes some of the **arid** areas in this hot plateau more fertile. Some types of grain are grown, mostly wheat and rice. Sheep and goats are also raised here.

The south and east
The warm climate of the south and east makes it possible for citrus fruit, grapes, and olives to be grown.

▼ Many farms in Spain have their own windmills to supply power for pumping water.

Amazing, but true!
Olives are one of Spain's most important crops, and they are grown all over the country.

Grapes for making wine are grown in most regions of Spain.

Cork is one of Spain's major products. Cork comes from trees and is used for making bottle stoppers, floor coverings, and bulletin boards.

The main crops grown on the Canary Islands are bananas and tomatoes.

Traveling through modern industrial Spain

Moving to the cities

Spain today is a modern industrial country. Over the last 40 years, many young people have left the villages in the countryside to look for work in the cities, where they can earn more money. More than 90 percent of Spain's population works in offices or factories.

As you travel around the Spanish countryside, you will notice that not many people live in rural areas now.

The capital

Madrid is a large city with a population of more than 3 million people. Madrid has a lot of manufacturing industries. Many people also have jobs in banking, business, and the media (for example, newspapers and television).

▼ About two million cars are made in Spain each year.

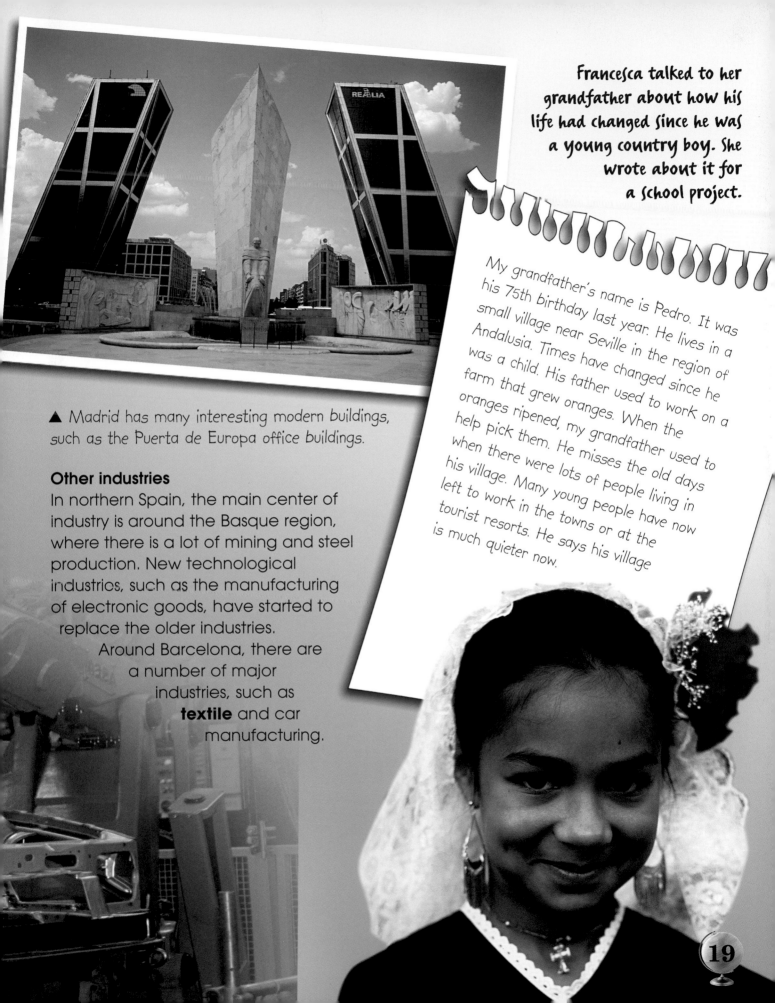

▲ Madrid has many interesting modern buildings, such as the Puerta de Europa office buildings.

Other industries

In northern Spain, the main center of industry is around the Basque region, where there is a lot of mining and steel production. New technological industries, such as the manufacturing of electronic goods, have started to replace the older industries.

Around Barcelona, there are a number of major industries, such as **textile** and car manufacturing.

Francesca talked to her grandfather about how his life had changed since he was a young country boy. She wrote about it for a school project.

My grandfather's name is Pedro. It was his 75th birthday last year. He lives in a small village near Seville in the region of Andalusia. Times have changed since he was a child. His father used to work on a farm that grew oranges. When the oranges ripened, my grandfather used to help pick them. He misses the old days when there were lots of people living in his village. Many young people have now left to work in the towns or at the tourist resorts. He says his village is much quieter now.

19

Festivals and traditions

Festivals in Spain

Spain is famous for its festivals, called *fiestas*. There is usually a religious theme, and the celebration normally starts with a church service.

There are several important dates when all the people in Spain hold celebrations. July 25 is Saint James' Day. Saint James is the patron saint of Spain, so there are fiestas throughout the country.

Regional festivals

Every region and town in Spain has holidays set aside for their own special fiestas. These fiestas often celebrate important people and events; for example, saints' days may be celebrated, or the successful harvesting of crops.

▶ Fiestas often include flamenco dancing, with men and women wearing colorful costumes and flowers in their hair.

▼ On special festival days, bulls are let loose in some village streets and people run along with them.

Bullfighting

Bullfighting is a popular form of entertainment in Spain. Some people believe bullfighting is cruel because the bulls are killed as part of the show. Others view bullfighting as an important part of Spanish culture. In Pamplona, a city in northern Spain, bulls are let loose in the streets during the Festival of San Fermín.

Traditional dancing

In southern Spain, there is a traditional type of dancing called *flamenco*. Men and women dance together. The men click the heels and toes of their shoes on the ground. The women wear colorful dresses and hold pairs of small wooden discs called *castanets,* which make clicking sounds.

Carlos wrote a postcard to his American pen pal about a religious fiesta in his region.

Dear Sam,
Today is March 19—St. Joseph's Day. In Valencia, there is a fiesta for carpenters. This is because Joseph, (who married Mary, the mother of Jesus) was a carpenter. Large statues are made from wood and wax, and prizes are given to the best ones. In the evening, people light bonfires and the sky sparkles with fireworks displays.
Carlos

Sam Wilson
3425 Redwood Road
Sunnyview, CA 92651
U.S.A.

▲ On St. Joseph's Day, the streets of Valencia are richly decorated with flowers and oranges.

Food and drink

▶ Tapas bars are very popular in Spain.

Spanish lunch

Traditionally, lunch was an important time for the whole family to gather together. The Spanish lunch, *la comida*, took place between 2 and 3 p.m. However, the fast pace of life in cities has made family lunches less common. The traditional main meal, if it happens, can be as late as 11 p.m.

Tapas

A popular food in Spain is *tapas*. It started as a small snack served in Spanish bars. It was provided as a light meal in the late morning to keep people going until lunch. Now tapas is served all day long and tapas restaurants can be found all over the world.

Regional dishes

The different regions of Spain have their own special dishes. Andalusia is famous for its seafood, and also for a cold soup called *gazpacho*, which contains tomatoes and garlic. In Catalonia, a popular meal is *oscalivada*, which is grilled vegetables, often served with grilled meat.

Wine

Spain is one of the largest wine producers in the world. The most famous wine it produces is *Rioja*. Sherry is a wine that is unique to Spain. It gets its name from the area where it is produced: Jerez in Andalusia in southern Spain.

▼ Mealtimes are an opportunity for the family to get together.

▲ Paella is a rice dish containing different meats and seafood.

Juan lives in Barcelona. Read about the different meals he has during the day.

For breakfast, I usually have bread with jam or jelly on it. School starts at 9:30 a.m. and ends at 4:30 p.m. I have a two-hour lunch break, so I go home and my mother makes lunch for me. My favorite is pasta in tomato sauce for the primero (first course) and for segundo (entrée) I like paella. For dessert, I have fruit. My father works at the car factory and does not get home until 8 p.m. We wait for him to come home before we have our dinner.

Tourism

How many tourists come to Spain?
More than 60 million people visit Spain each year. That is more people than actually live there!

Coastal attractions
Many people come to Spain to enjoy sunbathing on the beaches and swimming in the warm Mediterranean Sea. Coastal resorts stretch out along the eastern coastline from the Costa Brava in the northeast to the Costa del Sol in the southeast. Over the last 40 years, this coastline has been developed. Hotels, bars, nightclubs, and stores have been built. The islands of Spain are also popular with tourists.

▶ One of Spain's most famous churches is the Sagrada Familia in Barcelona.

Towns and cities
If you visit Spain, you can spend time enjoying the towns and cities in the interior. There are many well-preserved castles and buildings for tourists to visit. Madrid has famous art galleries and museums. Barcelona is another popular city for foreign visitors. It has unusual buildings designed by an architect named Antonio Gaudí. Perhaps the most famous of his buildings is the Sagrada Familia church. This building is known as "the sandcastle church" because of its shape.

The tourist industry

Many Spanish people have jobs that are created by the tourist trade. These jobs range from building hotels to working in them as waiters and maids. Tourism is the biggest industry for employment in Spain and has helped it become a richer and more modern European country.

▼ Many tourists enjoy the beaches on the Spanish Balearic island of Majorca.

Ben went to visit his Spanish pen pal. He wrote postcards to his grandma during his stay.

Dear Grandma,
I'm having a great time in Spain. We went to the beach yesterday and went swimming in the sea. After that we went shopping. There were some really great gift shops. I found a nice present for you—a traditional Spanish basket.

Love from Ben

Granny Neward
114 Evergreen St.
Palm Springs, CA
92651
U.S.A.

Environmental issues

Spain's natural habitats

Spain has a lot of land that has not been developed for people to live on. This means that **habitats** for rare wild animals have not been disturbed. Wild brown bears, wolves, and wild boars still live in the mountainous regions in the north of the country. In the warmer climates of the south, there are also rare animals, especially reptiles, which can live well in the weather there.

National parks

The increase in industrialization in Spain has placed important rare animal and plant life in danger. The Spanish government is attempting to preserve habitats for animals and plants in a number of **national parks**.

There are ten large national parks in Spain. The three most important are:

• Donana National Park in southern Spain. It provides a protected area for many species of birds. The last surviving lynxes (a type of wild cat) in southern Europe live here.

◀ Wild lynxes live in Donana National Park in southern Spain.

• Ordesa National Park is in the north and includes part of the Pyrenees. The only herd of *ibex*, the Pyrenean mountain goat, in the world is found in this park.

• Montaña de Covadonga National Park in northwestern Spain provides habitats for rare animals and birds such as the royal eagle.

There are more than 40 different kinds of orchids (a type of exotic rare flower) in the area.

Coastal development

The building of hotels and tourist attractions along the Mediterranean coast has destroyed some important sandy areas and **wetlands**. The Spanish government has placed stricter controls over development in these areas to protect the natural environment from further harm.

▼ Spain's national parks are meant to protect the natural environment from development.

Glossary

agriculture
farming the land to produce food

arid
dry, with low rainfall

coast
where the land meets the ocean

continent
a large area of land. There are seven continents in the world: Africa, Asia, Australia, Antarctica, North America, South America, and Europe

grazing land
areas of land covered with grass, where farm animals are kept

habitat
the natural home of a plant or animal

industrialized
area with many factories where a lot of manufacturing takes place

inlet
a narrow part of the ocean or a sea that comes farther into the land

interior
the central part of a country, not near the coast

irrigation
a method of storing and distributing water in order to grow crops

mainland
the part of a country that does not include its islands in the ocean

national park
area of land owned by the government where wild animals and plants are protected

peninsula
a piece of land almost entirely surrounded by water

plateau
a high, flat area of land

source
the place where a river starts

textile
cloth that is manufactured

toll
a cost that you must pay in order to use something; often a motorway

wetland
areas where the soil contains a lot of water

Index

Teaching ideas and activities for children

The **Travel Through** series offers up-to-date information and cross-curricular knowledge in subject areas such as geography, language arts, numeracy, history, and social studies. The series enables children to develop an overview ("the big picture") of each country. This overview reflects the huge diversity and richness of the life and culture of each country. The series aims to prevent the development of misconceptions, stereotypes, and prejudices, which often develop when the focus of a study narrows too quickly onto a small locality within a country. The books will help children gain access to this overview, and also develop an understanding of the interconnectedness of places. They contribute to children's geographical knowledge, skills, and understanding, and help them to make sense of the world around them.

The following activities promote thinking skills and creativity. The activities in section A are designed to help children develop critical thinking skills, while the activities in section B are designed to promote different types of learning styles.

A: ACTIVITIES TO DEVELOP THINKING SKILLS
ACTIVITIES TO PROMOTE RESEARCH AND RECALL OF FACTS
Ask the child to:
- Make an alphabet book for a young child, illustrating the contrasts in the regions of Spain.
- Research and investigate a mountain environment (the Pyrenees or Sierra Nevada) or a coastal environment. The child could present his/her information in a poster or a computer presentation.

ACTIVITIES TO STIMULATE UNDERSTANDING

Ask the child to:

- Use this book and other nonfiction books, CD-ROMs, and the Internet to find out about tourism in Spain. He/she can use this information to write a script for a TV travel program.
- Use this book and other sources of information to find out about industries in Spain (such as car manufacturing, wine and sherry production, or cork).

ACTIVITIES USING INFORMATION TO SOLVE PROBLEMS

Ask the child to:

- Make notes to explain the reasons why the regions of Spain have retained their own identities.
- Produce a poster advertising different types of vacations to Spain.

ACTIVITIES TO ENCOURAGE ANALYTICAL THINKING

Ask the child to:

- Compare and contrast life in Madrid or Barcelona with a city in the United States.
- Use reference books and the Internet to research the work of Gaudí and review the importance of his work as an architect in Barcelona.

ACTIVITIES TO PROMOTE CREATIVITY

Ask the child to:

- Look at pictures of Parc Guell in Barcelona and create a mosaic using small squares of colored paper.
- Research the work of Joan Miró (or Salvador Dalí or Pablo Picasso) and create a picture in that style using computer software or craft materials.

ACTIVITIES TO HELP CHILDREN USE EVIDENCE TO FORM OPINIONS AND EVALUATE THE CONSEQUENCES OF DECISIONS

Ask the child to:

- Write a report, giving reasons, why it is important to protect Spain's national parks.
- Make a list of five items that would best represent life in Spain.

B: ACTIVITIES BASED ON DIFFERENT LEARNING STYLES
ACTIVITIES FOR LINGUISTIC LEARNERS

Ask the child to:

- Write a rap to promote a Spanish Mediterranean coastal resort.
- Write a report about why people visit Spain for vacation, and the advantages and disadvantages for Spain of having lots of tourists.

ACTIVITIES FOR LOGICAL AND MATHEMATICAL LEARNERS

Ask the child to:

- Use reference books and the Internet to find out about the climate in the different regions of Spain and to show this information in a graph.

ACTIVITIES FOR VISUAL LEARNERS

Ask the child to:

- Select one place in Spain and design a visually appealing poster with a slogan that could be used to advertise it.
- Locate the major cities and rivers on a map of Spain.

ACTIVITIES FOR KINESTHETIC LEARNERS

Ask the child to:

- Design, plan, and help make a Spanish family meal.

ACTIVITIES FOR MUSICAL LEARNERS

Ask the child to:

- Dance the flamenco to some Spanish music.
- Create a short radio ad and radio station jingle to advertise a place or tourist attraction in Spain.

ACTIVITIES FOR INTERPERSONAL LEARNERS

Ask the children to:

- Write a letter to a child living in Madrid, explaining his/her own lifestyle (school, recreational activities, local area).

ACTIVITIES FOR INTRAPERSONAL LEARNERS

Ask the child to:

- Describe what he/she feels it would be like traveling on an AVE (high-speed tilting train) at up to 200 miles per hour between Seville and Madrid.

ACTIVITIES FOR NATURALISTIC LEARNERS

Ask the child to:

- Prepare a speech for a debate on the pros or cons of maintaining the national parks in Spain.